Black Faggotry

Dazié Grego-Sykes

NOMADIC PRESS

OAKLAND
111 FAIRMOUNT AVENUE
OAKLAND, CA 94611

BROOKLYN
475 KENT AVENUE #302
BROOKLYN, NY 11249

WWW.NOMADICPRESS.ORG

MASTHEAD
FOUNDING AND MANAGING EDITOR
J. K. FOWLER

ASSOCIATE EDITOR
MICHAELA MULLIN

DESIGN
J. K. FOWLER

MISSION STATEMENT
Nomadic Press is a 501 (C)(3) not-for-profit organization that supports the works of emerging and established writers and artists. Through publications (including translations) and performances, Nomadic Press aims to build community among artists and across disciplines.

SUBMISSIONS
Nomadic Press wholeheartedly accepts unsolicited book manuscripts. To submit your work, please visit www.nomadicpress.org/submissions

DISTRIBUTION
Orders by trade bookstores and wholesalers:
Small Press Distribution,
1341 Seventh Street
Berkeley, CA 94701
spd@spdbooks.org
(510) 524-1668 / (800) 869-7553

Black Faggotry
© 2020 by Dazié Grego-Sykes

All rights reserved. No part of this book may be reproduced or transmitted in any form or by any means, electronic or mechanical, without written permission from the publisher. Requests for permission to make copies of any part of the work should be sent to: info@nomadicpress.org.

This book was made possible by a loving community of chosen family and friends, old and new.

For author questions or to book a reading at your bookstore, university/school, or alternative establishment, please send an email to info@nomadicpress.org.

Cover artwork and author portrait by Arthur Johnstone

Published by Nomadic Press, 111 Fairmount Avenue, Oakland, CA 94611

First printing, 2020

Printed in the United States of America

LIBRARY OF CONGRESS CATALOGING-IN-PUBLICATION DATA

Grego-Sykes, Dazié 1977 –
Title: *Black Faggotry*
P. CM.
Summary: *Black Faggotry* by Dazié Grego-Sykes is a collection of poetry that loudly and proudly exclaims the intersectional realities of Black and Queer identities. These poems burst forth as raw catalysts toward transformational understanding. At times jarringly uncomfortable as truths often are, Grego-Sykes pulls no punches in consistently offering voice to the mutable nature of the QPOC experience.

[1. POETRY/QUEER STUDIES. 2. POETRY/AFRICAN AMERICAN. 3. AMERICAN GENERAL.] I. III. TITLE.

LIBRARY OF CONGRESS CONTROL NUMBER: 2019957647

ISBN: 978-1-7327866-8-4

Black Faggotry

Dazié Grego-Sykes

NOMADIC PRESS

for Derrick Miller-Handley

CONTENTS

INTRODUCTION

- 1   MIDDLE PASSAGED
- 3   THE CHANT
- 4   A SONG FOR THE NIGGAS
- 6   BLACK PRIVILEGE
- 12   A CHAIR IS STILL A CHAIR
- 16   NOTES OF A HALFRICAN AMBASSADOR
- 18   JIGABOO FAGGOT
- 19   FULFILLED INFILTRATION
- 20   REVOLUTION-REVELATIONS
- 23   MY BLACK MALE BODY
- 24   ANTEBELLUM DREAM
- 26   STRIPES
- 29   GRIFFEN
- 33   THE ATMOSPHERE OF A DREAM
- 35   MOTHS
- 36   A WINDOW, A TREE, A LEAF
- 37   I (UNTITLED)
- 40   DID YOU LIKE ME?

41	PEACOCK
42	MIST
43	THIS...
44	AFTER SUPPER
45	THE POND
46	MAGENTA
47	RED
48	BRIEFLY KISSED
49	KISS MY ASS
50	HEAVEN
51	LOVING HIM
52	TO KISS
53	AS SHE LAID
56	THE SANCTUARY
58	ACHE
59	WINGS
60	SWEPT AWAY
61	SLEEPING IN SADNESS
62	YOU CAN
63	COLOR STRUCK

64	STEPPING ON CRACK
65	HURRICANE CRACK
67	MAKE ME BLACK
	CLASSROOM GUIDE

INTRODUCTION

This book is the sound of my consciousness clearing its throat and speaking. I have opened myself up in order to explore some of the most profound experiences of my life. It is rare for me to sit down in front of a blank page and find myself composing anything upon command. I do not possess the gift of writing. This is a gift that possesses me. The words come so quickly that I have lost many poems looking for a pen. I catch it as it is born or it is lost. I have been seen running out of the shower naked and covered in soap all to capture a phrase that was flowing through my mind. These pages were all originally napkins, newspapers, hamburger wrappers, and grocery bags. These words are things I couldn't forget or had to remember, things I needed to share or make sense of. These words hit the page one letter at a time. They were mine and now they are yours.

I started writing this book when I began to see myself as an intersectional being. I am a place where roads from seemingly separate origins come together. In many ways, these poems are making sense of me, for me; when I stopped being one label at a time and instead experienced the sum of who I am. I stopped feeling the need to explain why I exist. As a biracial, Black, gay man, I am often asked, "What are you?" My response to that question can be found in the pages of *Black Faggotry*.

I've made the choice to include some of my earliest work in this book. This collection spans 1994–2019. Some of this work is pulled directly from solo plays I have written. Others can be found on my spoken word album, *Make Me Black*. I have placed them alongside one another to explore the larger narrative I have created not only as a performance artist, but as a poet. My poems are me broken down to my essence. They are not performative or contextualized by a single theme. They are there on the page awaiting a reader to give them meaning.

I write because it fulfills a need—a need to release paired with an even greater desire to be heard. My poetry is a tool, it is a mirror. I wonder what you will see when you first look at these pages? A revolutionary, a self-indulgent thinker, a vulnerable or courageous man?

MIDDLE PASSAGED

Born of cotton wombs
Softly whipped
       to coffin
Nappy hair to prune
       in hopes to stop the laughin'
Blistered foot is doomed
       to walk, another day
Uneducated tongue
       careful what you say
Broke shoulders spend your life
       hesitant but look
See not what holds today
       but prey for what's been took
We connect to our ancestors
       through the dialect we speak.
We protect our "broken English"
Our so-called poor grammar
       because more important than any language
       is the oral history we must keep.
It is swimming between our tongues
       and the very roof of our mouths.
It is an accent from Africa, United States
       North or South.

We are the children who have no written language
We hieroglyph pilgrims of the ocean
We voodoo prince
Eyes weeping willows
Green moss and forgotten days of mounting lions
       who still know our names.
They pace behind bars in zoos
Not unlike too many young Black brothers
The growls disturb the once sweet dreams
       we hear them under covers

Can't reach for the hand of God
        but passed the hand of Mothers
Hoard the love that's in your heart
        then look for some from others.

He thrashes his hips against his lover
Refuses to turn over
        and become receptive
Believes that death is born
        of absorbing
His lovers own dying seed
Nothing grows.
Wearing skin
        like withered leaves
Press your ear to my chest
Hear the mischievous wind
        left seeping,
        heart keeping,
        kisses left by breath
That cannot be perceived
Do not forget
        the beloved can always leave.
Water thrusts spilling blood of pirates
        with swords unsheathed
Froth on the shore
Un-drying saliva of African bones and names
        that will never be retrieved
I look to her call out "cousin"
        scream "uncle"
Cry do you remember me?
Ask was it the vessel, the ocean, or pale skins
        that stole you, from me?
No tears travel from the green in my Atlantic
        I middle passaged tenderly.

THE CHANT

> "A fight, a fight, it's a Nigga and a white.
> If the white don't win, we all jump in."

I was six years old, playing in the schoolyard the of Wheeless Road Elementary School in Augusta, Georgia, the first time I heard that chant. In my family, we were not allowed to say Nigger. I remember correcting another student and stating that Nigger was a bad word. He was white and he punched me in the chest, knocking the wind out of me. His friend, who was Black, encouraged him to beat me up and he did. I spent hours trying to decipher those words. I could not come up with any hidden meaning so I conceded that white people were not allowed to lose. I told my teacher that I had been beaten up and called Nigger. She said, "Well, aren't you?" I figured that they wouldn't have beat me up if I wasn't. Today I wonder if those white boys think, "Them Niggers is so dumb, they don't even know it ain't no good to be a Nigger." The most sophisticated insult is one the recipient is unaware of until the giver has left the room. These are the insults that sting twice. First you feel the jab that was intended. Second you feel the jab of being dumb.

The next time the other kids sang that song—"A fight, a fight, it's a Nigga and a white. If the white don't win, we all jump in"—I enthusiastically joined in. This time nobody hit me. There wasn't a fight at all. We just liked singing it. The words painted pictures in my mind.

Black boys, fighting white ones in the middle of chanting circles. The Black boy knows he has to lose, but still he fights hard.

A SONG FOR THE NIGGAS

I wanna sing a song
        about Niggas
I love me some Niggas
Every day
and all day
I be all Tupac
infused with Uncle Tom's nostalgia
For looking after white folks
whippings
and conveniently raping our wives
I didn't want to fuck that "ho" no way
I am sho nuff Nigga
Not a paid Nigga
        like Jigga
A no swagger having big
        lipped, coon
blue-black and shit and have no rooms
for things like education
I's sleep and eat
and penetrating
I's a Nigga, son
Got many children
ain't fathered one
You sho can tell
I go to church
        but live in Hell
So God bless the Niggas
This Nigga is disturbing
No house owning
but run the curb and
I'm proud to be a Nigga
I love when Niggas who ain't Niggas
        call they selves Niggas
Cuz I know they want to be me

They can't marinate on this big pimping
Saggy pants and steady limping

I got some color why you tripping?
Don't just say I'm penny pinching
What they call you while the lynching?
      Nigga?
      That's
who I be
I Amistad
Now give us free
Nigga.

BLACK PRIVILEGE

Why can't Black be a pretty thing?
an oh so, pretty thing
I wanna be pretty
"Black's not pretty
It's dirty, son"
Soiled as midnight
and toting a gun
I am your special guest
I have Black privilege
Ladies and gentleman
your very special guest.

My eyes are pretty
My skin is non-offensive
That won't get you down, brown
They call me mulatto
     meaning half and half
by definition it's a breed that cannot reproduce itself
That's bullshit
We call ourselves Black
You're mulatto
That's why you're brown
If you were Black
blue would accent your hue
Look how uppity you get
now who is talking 'bout who?

You think just because you're darker than me
you have a lease on pain.
You pay your dues
every day, like it's the first
Call yourself Nigga
then curse and curse.

You like your pain
Pain's not rent
Pain is a mortgage
You'd own a home by now
accept you're more interested in owning your pain
than owning a place to let go
No.
I'm sorry
Your pain owns you
Your pain destroys you

The reason, I call myself Black
is the reason
they call their selves white
We both want access to something

Are we "Brothas" or not?
We're Brothas when you want a cigarette.
Brothas,
when you need me to march with you?
Brothas,
when I was getting whipped next to you
I can't forget the one-drop rule

Bitch, don't be mad at me
cuz I can go where you can't
I am your special guest
Ladies and gentleman
it's your very special guest
Featuring NIGGAS.

Fists ask questions
white man's justice
never answers

The owl laid out in darkness
struggling against the moon
Asking
who?
who?
    who?
a clue?
Something ain't working out between me and you
Nigga-Roo.

I am a hybrid
That means I'm part monkey
but I always
always wanted to be pretty.
Instead, I ended up confused
As I take the light side or dark side of me
flip my coin
I'm in pleasure, half the time
They like to talk about my eyes
    how they are pretty
Yeah, I get to be *pretty*
Sometimes they call me Nigga and stare at me,
for a reaction

white people like to put their hand up
    and hold it next to mine
They say, "I am darker than you"
    like they've achieved something
I wish they'd try that shit with Yushica or Niasha
"Ishas" are dark skinned on resume paper
"Did they hire her or you?"
white people are funny
and disappointin'
Funny because in their natural state

they don't want to be offensive

In the U. S. A.
a red man's plain
offending is what they do best
I need a rest
from racism
I need to close my eyes
    sometimes
When it comes to white privilege
I am a distinguished guest.
I am so light
they don't' even frown
So light,
they're not offended
So light,
I am befriended
So light,
white people say things like
"Some people deserve to be called Nigger"
without blinking or
    thinking
Without even knowing, that as white as they are
    now they are showing me, their color
That's bizarre
White people must not have to think
Being Black
you think
Are they looking at me?
What do they think of me?
Do I speak good enough for them? I
mean well enough, for them
Should I speak at all?

I don't want to speak
I want to holler
I don't want to speak
I want to scream
I don't want to speak
I want to fight
I don't want to speak
I want to throw punch
I want to chew
I want to announce
my presence and my
       hatred
I don't want to be like you
I don't want to act civilized
       what you do, is not civilized
Why should I act like it's right?
What is right about being wrong?
Especially when being wrong
feels so white
I just want to be pretty.

There is no such thing as being Black
and being pretty
There's being Black
and being exotic
There's being Black
and being a slave
There's being Black
and being revolutionary
There's being Black
and being angry
There's being Black
and being a sellout
Black is not pretty

Black is not pretty
Black is beautiful
but not pretty.
I just want to be pretty
I am your special guest

Your very special guest
I am privileged,
to be Black.

A CHAIR IS STILL A CHAIR

Suffering is a choice
Pain is natural
To dwell on pain
    is to choose to suffer
Jealousy is founded in the fantasy
that someone else has
    what it rightfully yours.
Black is every color
Really black is any color
5 4 3 2 1
We are a part of a Nigga nation
Your burden?
Sit in your chair
    and wonder
How many Mexicans have died trying to get back here?
trying to get back home
Some people are so busy being Black
    that they can't be themselves.

What is Africa to me?
The water may not run clean
What is Africa to me?
The water may not run clean
What is Africa to me?
The water may not run clean
Kings and Queens
Kings and Queens
    What is Africa to me?
Kings and Queens
Kings and Queens
    What is Africa to me?
Martin Luther King
and Martin Luther King
and Martin Luther King.

I don't apologize for being
Why would I excuse myself?
As I cough up this disease
I don't say Ashé, but thank you
Won't you please
    listen to me?
I am not ashamed of this place
You love that my eyes are green
Colored like money
Colored like we paid
Colored like don't you forget, colored
    Nigga
Un-natural beauty is natural to me
Looka here at what we freed
It's the goodest hair
    dreadlocked with hypocrisy

Come on now, people
Let me hear you shout
I've been robbed
I ain't sold out
It weighs too much
Can't run and crutch
It's not algebra
Subtract the plus
Know what your people told
If you can't remember
Find yourself a Griot
This oral tradition
A sneaky suspicion
That this poet speaks unicorn
White folks can have history
    but then brown people get ancestry
Now you ask me,

    whose the child scorned?
The little brother
so quick to tattle
asking for mules
a crossbred cattle
A serpent's tail don't always rattle
Let's take a ride jump in my saddle

It hurts
that I have to make a conscious decision
    to date Black men
It hurts that I have to prove, I am worth loving
    by loving him
Having something to prove is a dangerous thing
Why else would it make sense?
To abandon our spirits to make cents?
It does make sense
That we refer to Africa
    in its pretense
But who among us believes
    that we can go back home
from where we are thieved
screaming, "What's been took from me"
Then give of ourselves on bended knee
    such beautiful hypocrisy
Shall we call out sacrilege?
While taking mental pilgrimage
You call it white man's privilege
He stole
    you ask to play with it
What, did you want to rape her first?
Oh, you wanted to rape her while she was still a virgin
It's okay baby
    we gon' go get the surgeon

Grow back her hymen
    you'll get your turn
Now is it gonna be okay?

Like my Great Granddaddy being a slave entitles me
Where are the reparations promised me?
Call this house a home?
Where is your key?
Buried, with the Cherokee?
"Chair aquí."
"¿Dónde está?"
"¿Comó se dice chair in Español?"
"Se dice, silla."

I see a room full of people
They are fighting over land
    that just don't belong to them
I see a Black
I see a white
I see a colonized American
We cannot go back home.

We who come in nakedness
We who cannot lie
even though it's in our own best interest

Suffering is a choice
Pain is natural
To dwell on pain
    is to choose to suffer

NOTES OF A HALFRICAN AMBASSADOR

White is not a race
it's a state of mind
the absence of color
It's where my shame was planted
The place my confusion blossoms
My African ancestors,
    pruning
    cutting back dead limbs
    stemming from ignorance
Contradicting pure bread
Creating biracial, bisexual
Slipping between dimensions
someone never wanted a man
    who was white
    to be Black
    to be gay
After tasting the fruit of women
Yes I've seen the light
But I stand in the shadows
Observing my people,
    all my people
The almond shaped eyes that display
    a hazelish
    reddish
    beige
Not simply one of the primary colors
I could find out what normal is
And I could love myself
for being a
    nappy-headed
    white-skinned
    green-eyed
    sissy
So I stand here

clutching my dual citizenship
never having a country
traveling from desert to oasis

JIGABOO FAGGOT

The jigaboo faggot, had much too much class
when he shook his ass
A dark skinned honkey
A pure-bred monkey
with eyes like mongrels have

FULFILLED INFILTRATION

I cross my legs
merely to offer you
a fulfilled expectation
The rising vibrations
    of words
that mean cruel things
And I am hearing faggot again
the equivalent of less than man
Because I can
hold him in my arms
I can liquefy his skin
churn him into cocoa butter
pacify the pain of Brothas
heal and cool
    the heat of others
I can infiltrate a man

REVOLUTION REVELATIONS

You say you want a revolution
Your heart and words keep producing
inspiration, leading nation
yet I've seen no contemplation
laying here invisibly
only seen through HIV
Your mind and eyes refuse to see
butch bull dykes dethroned by He

If you claim her only worth
is playing wife and childbirth
it's confusion, role is lost
You judge and joke then Bible toss

Quick to braid and dread your hair
Read history through closed-eye stare
Preach my brothas, burn your sages
all the while skipping pages
Spouting off 'bout Nefrititi
Intellect smoked out on bidis

Looking here to present thrones
you'll notice royal families grown
Don't act like you haven't seen
standing here is modern Queen

When this revolution comes
pretending righteousness was done
will you condemn like other ones?
telling all that you're oppressed
yet what you say's heterosexist

Weren't you told cuz I believe
there's no boundaries in unity

Racism made it OK for lynching
don't just say I'm penny pinching

For all your wordless silent action
say you never went gay bashing

We are problem or solution
Watch them laugh accept illusion

Yes I swish and I ki ki
but baby boy don't play with me
Don't you know?
     I plainly see
my misplaced role
     society

They say he's straight
get him wet he'll bend
What kind of message does this send?
Call the hate, homophobic
extreme dislike for claustrophobics

Cuz we couldn't live in box
You act like we got chicken pox
What you think that gay's contagious?
recruiting folks that shit's outrageous

Pointing fingers always judge
take God's words and quickly smudge
You're talk'n 'bout Leviticus
some twisted words ridiculous
It's all about some hypocrites
don't think I will get into it

Search out revolutionist
Don't look past limp-wristed fists
You might find your adversary
is the boy you called a fairy

We must overcome facade
It's not about who gets my rod
Maybe we have sealed our fate
because it's you we'd never date

There's much more to identity
then just queer sexuality
So why's it all that you can say is
"Yeah he's cute, but girl he's gay."

MY BLACK MALE BODY

My Black male body does not belong to you. It is not yours. It will not submit under whip or word. My Black male body's purpose is not to further your personal or political agenda. You cannot liberate me. The idea that you can contradicts the concept, that I am already free. I am not a savage to domesticate or a slave to repossess. I am not an underdog because I've been passed your test. My Black male body is not in prison. My Black male body is not contained. My Black male body exists here. My Black male body exists now. My Black male body exists for itself and because of itself.

My Black male body is male. My Black male body is male. My Black male body is intimidating. My Black male body is strong. My Black male body is fighting you. I am not Martin Luther King Jr. I am Jason, Damien, Khalil. I am that Nigga over there. I am indicated by your fear. My Black male body is Black. My Black male body is brown. My Black male body is tan. My Black male body is pale. My Black male body is fooling you.

I am not a movement, a waste, or failed potential. I am not a weapon, an excuse or a grave. I am what I am, who I have been, I am who I need to be. I am Sambo. I am Zip Coon. I am Mandingo and I, is pretty. My pain is not a canvas. My history is not a primer for your guilt. I am not a magnifying glass, you will not see yourself through me. You can never fire me because you never hired me. You cannot buy me or reimburse me for my labor. I am not an African. I am not a *New Negro*, I am not a poem, romanticize yourself. Clearly that's what you're used to. I am here for you. I am here to be something other than you. Something for you to hate. Something at which you can marvel. I am not yours. I am not supposed to be. Not hardly, not ever, not possibly, not in any light, at any time, in whatever dimension, string theory'd distraction from the now-ness that is me. You got exactly what you wanted. I am an obstacle, a grudge, an improvisation.

ANTEBELLUM DREAM

He has nothing
His Blackness is a figment of white imagination
He is the cold and tortured shadow
    of white folks past
One light
One dark
Each founding the other's weakness
Catch me if you can
Man.

He fucked my woman
He fucked my woman
He fucked and fucked my woman
I am not a man.

Yeah nigga, I fuck
I beat that pussy up
I fuck my woman
I fuck my woman
I fuck all woman
Clutch my swelling cock
On street corners
Primary weapon
Your perception
I big dick
Nigga joke
A yoke
And drag my masculinity behind me
This should all be far behind me
I stick it to my skin
With precamed fantasy of blood
    and white women's vaginal secretions
I beat her pussy up
She needs to suffer for what she's done to me

by liking this Mandingo-ism prism
They hold it up to the light
It's white
Out of me pours color
Never for be seen
I so Black
This antebellum dream

STRIPES

They want to take away my stripes
Call me sir
Hand me wife
A camouflage-less jungle beast
Hunted by lovers and others for feast
I am the color of light
the shadow of invisibility
I been running through this
gay black
Black gay
trade, Queen, Ms. Thang

Been reaching for the arms of brothers
needing a fortress
needing some cover
more than a friend
less than a lover
wanting someone with palms the color of Cocoa Krispies,
    to apply some kind of ointment
to a battered soul and blistered feet
I been running and dodging
but words keep on lodging
stifling my mentality

Can't help but feel the indigestion
Asked to keep my lover with discretion
Handing me out moral lesson
You're not the father who you testing?

It's time to get deeper
I mean penetration
like Lauryn Hill said
it's miseducation

Told me its crystal
In truth, it's just glass
Hear the bell ringing?
Gay black history class

Our ancestors refer to gay as divinity
Modern men still prefer terms like "failed masculinity"
crossing their torso and praying to trinity
whoring their God's word and claiming virginity

My philosophy
might seem to be
complex but it's simplicity
Won't sell my soul
or pay your toll
I am the man
I claim my role

Downplay my identity
Define my sexuality
Devalue my validity
Turn straight white male to currency

Once dues are paid and bed is made
reality leaves feelings played
can't count how many straight boys laid
retracing facts I'm clocking trade

They tasting my precum
laid out on their tum tum
straight tossing the bum bum
and eaten the dim sum

Take away my stripes?
Use words to verbally castrate me
Use clubs too literally "Castro" me
The land where bomber jackets are uniforms
and CK-1 is worn like nigga repellent

Street soldier
Pink Panther
Vaccine this gay cancer
Cleaning out
Names they shout
Want the tea
Tilt my spout

Revolution is revealed
The kind of fruit you'll never peel
Contains the meat that you can feel
The most satisfying meal

They wanna take away my stripes
They wanna
Matthew Shepard me
They wanna
Brandon Teena he
They wanna
Rodney King the homosexuality

Steal my stripes
I'll take them back
Like drag queen and hair weave
I'm right on track

GRIFFEN

I knew the word was mighty when…
Griffen
That man
That man who wore skirts
Simple cotton fabrics
and neutral tones of crème or brown
At 6 foot 3 inches he was a tower
to this post-adolescent
     pre-man
Me just 17
That's one month after a dick in my hand meant love
Not just a relapse back to Boy Scout camp
I stood
     shaking
Shaken because what I was seeing in this man
     was what my grandmothers had
Contagious laughter
A voice smooth and harmonious
Breath that smelled like home
Because a life of
     barbecues
     cocoa butter
     ultra sheen
     and prayer
Had nestled into the cracks of those battered lips
Lips that kissed
     small nieces and nephews
Lingering on foreheads longer than any auntie or mother dared
Because he understood that they could not be his children
Lips that licked
     tears from cheeks and bleeding knuckles
That were meant to hold
But were forced into protecting from would be
     cousins

      brothers
      lovers
      and friends
Lips that parted and separated
      inviting
      accepting
      entertaining
      giving pleasure
      swallowing small tremors
Lips that prepared and cleansed phallic extensions
moments before they pushed into a warm place you must feel to believe
And when condoms broke or found their way into bed corners couch crevices or wallets in jeans on floors
Places that may as well have been foreign countries
Grasping the moment seemed
Common sensual
      see he needed that thing in him
He needed that thing now
Not now
but right now
Yes, these words are mighty
but love is ruled by Aphrodite
So a year later when he had swollen glands and morning sickness he knew
He knew like all sissies turned Queen know
His man hadn't given him small foreheads to kiss but his own to place cold cloths upon
Straight girls get babies, faggots get AIDS
He never asked for revenge or clichéd phrases
What goes around really does come around
But never from those lips
Me just 17, not knowing the word, myself or of shared experiences
thought this man who wore skirts
      that lacked flamboyancy
      could not be touched by my own simplicity

He never asked to hear though I read

I felt his touch again at last
Closed my eyes and remembered what once was
Rejoiced and mourned the presence of his love
as arms and legs tangled in darkness
I felt his skin
The warmth of his breath
    suffocating me
    pacifying me
    loving me
One more night
I watched him sleep
Knowing when the sun rose
he would no longer be mine
In lust I ignored tomorrow's pain
The moonlight began to fade
As the sun slowly crept up the blankets onto his face
I held him
Closed my eyes and remembered
I will never again forget
Getting up I kissed his lips
sucked in the mourning air
resenting the sun once more
I looked to him lying peacefully
Wondering if it was too late to have him awake in my arms
where he would be overcome by my love for him
And know
this is where he belongs
He awoke
my fears became reality
I watched him rub the sleep from his eyes and me from his soul
But I remembered
    Love.

Finished and looking up from my first journal
I saw those eyes like grandmothers have doing what I thought they could not do
He cried
So when I read that poem I knew he believed in
new beginnings
second chances and lives lived in something
other than vain
He chose
He chose to fill me with the foundation of those tears while eating his own
cynicism

"And I'm not a jaded old queen," he said.
"And yes I played dueling dicks and lost"
"And pick and choose your battles baby"
Yes he called me baby
Called everyone "baby"
Called grown men years older than him baby
and they accepted it the way a child says nothing when called
Beans, Peanut Butter, Deb Deb, or Pooquie
"Have your lines ready," he said, then baby again
"And when he ain't loving you
you love you
but don't give in
don't think
don't ever think
you have to know
them hearts always beat again."

THE ATMOSPHERE OF A DREAM

It swims, cool and reflective. Vibrantly colorless, saturated and introspective. Be here now, at least for a little while. No matter how present you are it's impossible to know if you will remember a single thing. Spider webs with no spiders, silkworms playing with their friends. It is nothing. It is crisp. It is absent and bright. It's the end and the beginning. It is everything because it is. There's no point in waiting around here. No point in traveling down pale cotton candy lined streets. You will not meet the inhabitants. Somehow you've always known who they are. This is your infinite everything. If a word must first be a thought before it's spoken into being, then these are not words. These are mad ramblings of a fumbling God. Now you can fly. You will always catch the ball. These words are things. Things that may be received by a man who wants to be changed by the quality of words.

This is a place where thoughts are ever-changing their form. They morph at a speed undetectable to the human eye, so you close them and venture back into your mind. There is room here for every universe. Sometimes a star will walk on by not concerned with who you are. Not bothered that you are a man. Not bothered that you can only ever be jealous. You wished to see it up close and now none of your former wishes apply. Constellations are inconsiderate things. Things are considered and deconstructed. Remember, this is a place where words are thoughts and thoughts are things. Don't puzzle yourself with stars, sherbet or red doors. You don't get to know, you do get to wonder. Wonder up a marvelous thing. Wander down any corridor. Open any drawer. You get the feeling, the gist, and the desire, all pressed between your mind and an intergalactic sky.

Stars are allowed to get tired of being wished upon, tired of pushing light into the cornea. Tired of looking stationary just because it eases your mind. Stars know who they are. They know that you will never see beyond your own sun-dotted confusion. Refreshed, born over and over again. Always being born. Never finding time to die. There is no time in this place, time is absurd. You could connect it all to a single second, first, you have to find one. Seconds are rare, they breed in time.

How long is a lifetime in an atmosphere without time? There isn't so much to know, there is plenty to believe. Beliefs are not thoughts, they are ideas. Ideas are free. Ideas can change. Ideas are ideas. Knowing is an earthly thing. Knowing is an atom bomb, a forest on fire, an eyelash that scratches out the eye of its host. Remember this is an atmosphere. This is not a place.

MOTHS

You are giving me moths
fragile
wise
albino.
A butterfly held
is a butterfly lost.
Butterflies do not stay.

I stand.
I kneel.
tattered intestine
I fall
fluttering wings on my breath
Sacred woolen heart
        protect me
Let me feed him some more.

A WINDOW, A TREE, A LEAF

Solemn twisted
Swaying tree
Shedding bark
Dropping leaves
Scattered children
Never found
A dance
A twirl
And then the ground.

I (UNTITLED)

I found all those tears from midnights when I was holding beer bottles and cigarettes instead of loving myself.

I found the prison I accepted when I chose to allow white powders with little consistency and many crystals to create feelings of freedom, simultaneously trapping me.

I found, I am finding. I am looking down at the ground. I've sunk my feet in and I barely recognize my own shoes. I found rationalization protecting, no, convincing my mind that I did not choose this. And I remember that beer in my hand, straw in my nose, bump in my ass, dick in my mouth.

I sound out the vowels and consonants. I hear words, sentences, phrases. My pen is moving ink is flowing.

I sound like a man who has realized his name is not what his Mama calls him but what God will let him be.

I sound, I am sounding. I wonder what trust is really for, dependable things never bend while others always will. You have either or are awaiting an opportunity that promises enough gain for you to make sense out of abandoning love. I only offered myself and personal growth. I've choked. I make no sound.

I see clouds before you and fasten my coat. I anticipate darkness because night air is capable of hiding and drying my tears. Tears that moonlight makes sparkle, making art out of God's canvas.

I see God everywhere watching me look for more than the color purple. Watching me, God I see.

I see, I am seeing. I saw the look in a young man's eye who felt astonished by the realization that I would cause him pain. He believed my experiences with pain made me wise. He believed my pain would protect him. I no longer see anyone.

I feel the sun warming, burning, warning me. I've touched hot only wanting that pretty flame to be my hand. Now I am holding blisters.

I feel pain, more pain, pulsating reproducing itself. Choosing a seat in my parlor binging on sadness and remixed old school love songs gone wrong. Gone wrong in content. Gone wrong in the assumption it could be remade, and I remember the first time I heard that song.

I feel, I felt like calling you the one. Making you the one but love can't transform spirits. Love is what it is, will not pretend for me.

I taste my mother's kitchen inventions and know she went hungry more than once to feed the greed of a child's mouth that held more lust for flavor than the stomach has elasticity.

I can still taste tequila from my brother's 21st birthday and can't imagine what it would have meant to take my first communion.

I taste. I am tasting like lemonade sweet but unnatural.

I smell his cologne. And his cologne. And his cologne.
I smell un-oiled church pews, the sweat of an upper lip calling on the Holy Spirit. Warding off Satan. Quivering, Moving, Yelling, Praying

I smell, I am smelling stale cigarettes smoke on freezing knuckles and I always wanted but never purchased gloves.

I hear cupid masturbating shooting me with jism and not arrows.

I hear what blind people can't see and now I'm frightened of the world.

I hear, I am hearing toes picked and finger licked but the dawn is in my past.

I am a ghetto prophet in suburbia. Here I am not wise.

I am, I am not

I'm am-ing, I be.

DID YOU LIKE ME?

Did you like me?
The tight young ass
The smoothness of my not yet ripe pee-pee
Were the pleasures you stole
worth the pain I keep?
Was the blood an adequate lubricant?
Your thrust
did so much more than fill me
I swear
it killed the
Sparkle of my eyes
My freedom to try
The experience of first times
My nose was stained with the smell of cum
Before I had become
Capable of wet dreams
Did I like it?
Are you the one who trained me?

PEACOCK

I strut like peacock with broken feather
single plume, beaten weathered
flawed altered incomplete
Phoenix bird, pigeon feet
sunless moon, blackened pure
organic fruit, Apple core
stormy night, acid rain
youthful soul gripping cane
child rests
molested bed
ravaged soul
twisted head

MIST

How did I get here?
Standing in the mist
dancing upon thistle toe
burning lover's kiss
shedding skin and training eyes
contemplation multiplies
I swore to self
this heart had died
within your arms
I'm proud to lie.

THIS...

This world seems like a cruel place to be
A container for suffering
and any translation or product of misery
Pandora's box was neither opened or freed
Its hate rage sadness and envy secured within me
I bite my tongue
chew my flesh
swallowing blood so no one sees
I've tamed my pen
Attempt to never unharness any form of cruelty
this bone and flesh
this box
this head
this world I live

AFTER SUPPER

She looks up at me from a sink full of dish water. Unexplained tears in her eyes. She still washes dishes by hand. The dishwasher serves no purpose in her house. The dishwasher takes up space, The dishwasher wastes water and soap. Life is hard she says, Life is very very hard. I ask if I can help. I know that I can't. I know that she won't let me wash her dishes. I know that she expects me to understand why. The dishwasher makes noise. The only way to be sure something is clean is to clean it yourself. After all this time those eyes have never dried.

I make her laugh again. I make her laugh because my heart is breaking. I make her laugh realizing that quickly too quickly the laughter will subside. For seconds pain is forgotten . The laughter only reminds her to ask, "When are you leaving?" I don't answer. Again, she cries. "I don't want you to go," she says. "I have to go," I say, "I have to go and get what's mine." She looks down at the dish water. I can't see her face. Her right hand trembles and I can literally see small splashes made by her tears. I am speechless. I don't cry. I don't ever cry. I haven't cried since the day he left. Since I stopped trying to die. As I look back at her face, I notice she is staring ever so still. "You're thinking of him aren't you?" I smile; I smile like a teenage boy caught masturbating. I smile because for her this isn't a surprise. I smile because from her I can never hide. She dries her hands crosses the room takes down a collage of photos and removes a picture of me holding him from the wall. "You have to forget," she says. "Just forget." I look away as if not seeing the photo would hurt less. I look at the dish water, put my hands in and cry. Only when I am in pain does she say my birth name, only when I am deeply in pain. I busy myself, these dishes need cleaning, I busy myself, the rag needs wringing. I busy myself. She doesn't try and stop me. Instead she lights me a cigarette, places it in the ashtray and says, "I'll wash, you dry."

THE POND

I find myself in unfamiliar surroundings. Staring at a large pond as it billows steam into a crisp September morning. I am thinking of a great many things and wondering about my Father. He would be at home in this place. Crickets standing on their porches yelling for their kids to come home. Dragonflies glistening like a woman's freshly glossed lips. Cold, cold air interrupted by the Sun's warning to all below. Today will be hot and the pond will be full of every and any species of life that wants to be cool.

I find myself at a familiar entry point in uncommon surroundings. The unrest of insects. The friskiness of my pet. The wind disrupting silent leaves, creating millions of sounds in a single second. I am feeling small, this just might be the point. Allowing my petty and vain concerns to evaporate like the morning dew. The grass looks like it is on fire. I see smoke, I smell nothing but clean air and immediately stop writing to light a cigarette. I grin and acknowledge the hypocritical being that is reminded to smoke by a clean breeze, an invisible stream I feel but never see.

I wonder about my Father. I am silent. My silence returns me to my origins. How did I arrive from all the chaos to a place of clean sounds and penetrating winds? What will I say when I finally return home? Most days I am half a step away from tears. Tears of extreme gratitude. A baptism for my cheeks. This holy place on my face, that a child might kiss, my dog might lick, that a lover, god willing will caress. Just half a step away from tears but I do not move forward. I will not move the tears from the corners of my eyes to the corners of my mouth. Tears love to wait on corners. Saline hoodlums that gather, collect salt and spit without a care for where their wetness lands.

I am imagining my Father. Lips pressing downward as he swallows his own smile. Eyes beaming with the curiosity of a playing child. Getting ready to speak with a slight hesitation. "I'm talking about you, not me when I say this." I am talking about you, thinking about you, imagining you are here preparing to leave the pond and walk with me down a long and dusty trail.

MAGENTA

Magenta in October
The dusk of perception
Androgynous,
two spirits synchronized and divine
She is mother earth
wombless womanhood
masculinity divide
milkless Madonna
Her eyes cry

RED

Turn insecure
My confidence
and still this love is pure
pink bunnies
in pastels
Green eyes
sweet smell

My heart is whining of
purple sands and possibilities
black ocean, blue skies
Color this, red thighs
blinking with wonder
and a heart that sings
for only you
Sings a beautiful melody
charming, exquisite
forming relationship

BRIEFLY KISSED

As you lick me there
sucking, embracing
closed-eye stare
I'm learning for whom these lips were formed
My mouth is dancing
hearts entrancing
intertwining
becoming you
one moment floating
lips demanding
briefly kissed
now I'm standing

KISS MY ASS

I love a man
who has the audacity to fuck me with his tongue
all the while
talking shit
This one time, literally
he be tasting me
on the inside part
like hungry infant
I momma
and yeah, I call out "Daddy"
I translate what sounds like a mumble
but feels like annunciation.
Sometimes he make midnight snack
out my ass
Like he mosquito
I wake up itchin'
knowing I been bit
He play like
he sleeping
I awake
Now, I be needing it
I ask why he likes it him say
is warm
is smooth
is good
I say, some folk think it nasty
He says
he not nasty
Tells me
    "fuck you"
Me say
    "kiss my ass"
and then
his dick grow.

HEAVEN

Don't look up to a moonless sky
Don't say prayers when infants die
I'm standing in God's waiting room
Attended by satan's stewardesses
I fly
so high
Heaven is not here.

LOVING HIM

Sex has become my way of shunning love
my way of saying fuck you
while I am fucking him
I didn't mean to give in
but I meant to give
so I gave
and it was too much
Waiting
Hoping
Praying
Worshipping a man who would not appreciate me stating his name
and he was not God
but I might of convinced him he was
while I was loving him

TO KISS

To kiss my cheek
is to bless a tear
to feel a pulse
to track my fear
and breath harnessing and pen
and ear containing

I blistered
I callused my own lips
I locked suffering between my tongue
      and the roof of my mouth
So no one kissed me
So my mother is the only one
who remembers the softness of my lips
So I held back to protect you
sacrificing my deepest need
Kiss me, kissing me, kissed…kisses…kissed.

AS SHE LAID

She said I want to be saved
as she laid
in makeup smears and infant tears
white pillows turn to grey
half perm in head
frayed split ends dangling from a 16-year-old mentality
sore and callused nipples seemed to be bleeding not feeding
The bastard child with whom she laid
but she stayed
wanting to be saved

The man she ever so affectionately called her nigga had just walked in
with Seagram's gin
she thought was Tanqueray

Tossing his head
quickly glancing
silently acknowledging
gin and tonic-ing
universally ebonicing
greetings and salutations
Leaving her to contemplate

Probing with a smile
she passively questioned
what were his intentions?

Had he come with aggression
or filled with depression
The reply found its way to her already swollen lips
on the wings of fists
tear-camouflaged eyes
trembling voice pleading why
She discovers the clotted white mucus flowing down her chest

as baby gurgled in vomit

She was finally standing
longing for freedom
staring at her self-proclaimed savior
the one she needed saving from

The heat of the water has caused her untasted juices to flow
She sighed
take me away
as she laid

Sliding in porcelain
romantic-less bubbles
hearing her troubles
as junior rested his head against the breast of nanny

The man of her house
The husband
The spouse
Was attending another conference
leaving her to coordinate
the cocktail parties and social events
all of which were necessary in order to present illusions
The upper-class solution
to divorce

Hair and makeup technician
Fumbling through *Mademoiselle* and *Vogue*
Turning to fashion and trend
The MAC pen stick and white pencil
ceased to disguise
crescent-shaped bruises that cradled her eye
the Calgon had collected

gritty like sand and irritating her privacy

She was,
finally standing
longing for freedom
opting for some form of psychiatry
resenting legalities
and prenuptial agreements

They say
they lay
entrapped by circumstance
One waits for "Captain Save a Ho"
the other teases her best friend's husband inappropriately
neither suspecting or seeing
the possibility of second-hand beatings
the cycle repeating

And she said I want to be saved
and she sighed take me away

THE SANCTUARY

There is a fly I've never met
licking my arm
Salt
Be it mine
or be it misted
    by the ocean
I've seen her
turquoise and blue
    in some far-off destination
But home
    she is grey like me
here and only here
    she is comfortable
She is all of herself
She is sharks
    both white and great
Is concrete hard for those who leap
Some people do jump off bridges
    and live
I could be swallowed whole by water or wind.
Once you're chewed it makes no difference
This golden-gated destination
is the final one for those who want to be high
even if it lasts just for seconds
Father Times filthy boots
pressed
    and kicking
The horizon and the mind.

The ancient waves giggle
away
Toss centuries-old boulder
until it's flour fine
    like the flour men

She burns, she browns, she tans
The Black ones play near
not in
They say we can't tread water
We say
if what happened before
    happens again
we'll go much free'er if we can't swim
We are living monuments
much too close to the massacre
Our bones are made of the ones who lived
Our skin is heavy and bronzed
We do not sink but run to the ocean floor
to greet our family and friends

You are here frolicking
I am here feeling small
My mind like water
    drifts
like wood
tightening in my shorts
It's good to grow

An empty throne
A tomb worshiping pagan
An absent mirror
Seeing without a seer
into my womb
My virgin sanctuary
    quietly
There I was
microscopic cosmic shard
on the tongue of a bug
I came to know

ACHE

Needle.
Point.
Pinch.
A rip that stings.
pain has gone to sleep
There is just one cell awake
      just one feeling on repeat.

ACHE,
Deep
So deep that it's everything.
Can't be cuz like bone
it's holding onto something.

Take,
Advice like borrowed recipes
Bake them a dish they'll like
this invention is not yours
      but still
it is in your home.

Fake
an orgasm in pushy bottoms hole
it's this or be alone
punch the place that hurts
thank the distraction.

and glance at your face again
confirm that
it
ain't
lasting.

WINGS

All I have
is a single feather
to prove I once had wings
My satin skin
has turned to leather
a throne without its King
I still remember
from what I come
a paradise has turned to slum
I'm sober now
but taste the rum
A wine is drank
fermented plum.
look for me at dawn
in dusk
wearing smoke
like Jovan musk
A blown-out speaker
hear Sade sing
to the crippled fairy
that burnt his wings

SWEPT AWAY

First they look because I am beautiful
Then they stare
      seeing how uncomfortable
      my beauty makes me
If I could only peel back my skin
These are my secrets
This is the sound of snickers
sliding between fangs
Their origin, insecurity
but you prefer that they are
      in me
I can't defend myself
I won't risk making you feel
      how I feel right now
I wonder if you know how
This is for the ugly little girl
      who hoped and hoped
Searching for what's beautiful
      she smoked and smoked
No matter how hard she swishes
      her hips aren't wide enough
Ruby slippers can't be less big
Drowning in the wake
      of her own step
she's swept
away.

SLEEPING IN SADNESS

Sleeping in sadness.
breath is not breath
Air sits, stale in lungs
Stomach turns.
Sad memory
Ashamed memory
God forgive me.

breath...

When this happens.
When there are no more episodes
No more season whatever on Netflix
Now, I lay me.
Some kind of colored
      embarrassed
ridiculousness.
I ask myself
if this is it.
Scroll postings on Facebook
      into nothingness.
Cruel glass laughs.
tells me this was always the plan.
The time kept safe on my watch
      tic or toc the drum does mock.
Peculiar marching band.
I say go graceful and easy.
I say Eleanor Rigby was on to something.
I know that now, it is my turn.
I hear a strangely familiar voice say,
Show me what you learned.

YOU CAN

You can't see or feel what I am
Why can't you
see me
see me here now
Unable to start mourning because I lost something
      unable
Why can't we
stop hiding and heal each other
You are my sweetest dream
but you can't
Why can't
      why not why
Why am I here again
I know this place
this was home and I left
No I ran
never meaning to return
You've called me back to my place of origin like a sick mother
I can
I have
I am
I am returning for you
hoping that now you can see
see this, feel this
I need you
I need something
I am not this tragic
I am
I am happy and loving
and you
you
see this
you take this
you can

COLOR STRUCK

Dark skin
Black man
Ashy
Choking on his own nappy hair
Wide nose
Fat lips
Afrocentric
Hey tar baby
I see the light-skin brothers with their good hair and green eyes
laugh as they pass you by
muttering names like shadow, spot and jigaboo
What they thinken?
You weren't no better passing them calling out half-breed, mutt, and Oreo
one of you thirsty for more color
the other too eager to give it away
A white man drives by in his shiny BMW
A racist laughs all he sees is niggas
Black skin, brown, yellow and tan got to embrace each other
Color struck

STEPPING ON CRACK

Step on a crack
break your momma's back
kids in the yard won't cut you no slack
walking down the street thinking back
but nowadays crack is wack

Little man thinks he's grown
stomps the pavement with careless tones
somewhere far his momma moans
Seeds you plant
Seeds you've sown

I should go back to simple days
I should rewind the song I play
Should remember not to stray
Play your game and youth will stay

Steppin On Cracks
Steppin on Crack
Steppin On Cracks
Steppin on Crack
Steppin On Cracks
Steppin on Crack.

HURRICANE CRACK

At first, I thought they called it crack because that's what it did to people's teeth. They smoked little white bits, sacrificing one tooth at a time. And then repeat. They dug holes into their faces right where their smiles should be, leaving pipe wiped soot streaked across their skin. They dug holes and planted bodies like infectious seeds, now only suffering can grow.

Remember that time Pooquie looked at himself upside down in a powdered covered mirror and asked that fateful question. "I wonder what it's like to be high?" and how getting high brought him so low that when the hurricane crack got here there was nowhere lower left to go?

That was back when he still had everything. Before his wife left and his momma died. Back when it made sense that he called himself clinging to his pride. He too high to know, that clinging to your pride don't mean that shame can't grow. Maybe if his shame got here before the police, his kids would still have a daddy and wouldn't have taken up slangin on their own. That's just how it is. Folks gotta eat, just like other folks gotta sit there watching the news while people like us become it. Emancipated good girls and emaciated toss-ups mumble, "I'll suck ya dick, for a hit."

On these streets, you might get slapped for saying anything less. No one here is desirable but all are available. Everyone except the dealer that is. He's cooked up baking soda and candy cane, unleashing the most tremendous Hurricane through Pooquie and em's home. At Pooquie's, lips are ash white, fingertips are blistered, and thumbs are callused from the never-ending flicking of BICs. Babies diapers are full of shit, screen doors are cracked open with porn or day time soaps blasting at the most absurd volume.

Gaping Black mouths, Burnt lips. Chapped lips, Curled, twisted and absolutely cracked lips. Crack was meant to be a sound, the fearful tone of breaking bone. And a single mother just invented a newborn that can't be rocked to sleep. Crack rocked the cradle. Was it an intact Black home that bothered the nation? Some of us are old enough to remember when these streets were still clean. Clean like Mrs. Johnson said she'd get. Rehab is real but the Re-habit is realer. How you supposed to get clean the CIA is your dealer. *Deliberate bloodthirstiness, relaxed, barbarity, unhurried, brutality. Slow Violence*

MAKE ME BLACK

Make me Black. Paint me. Be sure and make it obvious. My lips should be full. My hair, exceptionally curly. I want each strand wound so tight that if I fell down the steps I'd become a "slinky". My eyes, almond shaped and somewhat slanted. I am not sure if that is African, or Native American. Make them deep set and slanty. Take my oral tradition and forget it completely. Write down what you remember. Take my worth, multiply it by Nefertiti then divide it by crack whore. If you have a remainder, snap your fingers to your own heartbeat, roll your neck once and spit every time you want to say Nigga. Allow me to imitate you after you've made caricatures of me. Embarrass me, have me make fool after fool of myself and when I'm done giving it coon show, Halle Berry me.

Whisper Maya Angelou poems to the leaves, crush them. Make sturdy pages I can write my "Nigga songs" on. Tell me I am not Black if I am articulate, especially if your blue eyes are taken for granted. If your blue eyes are taken for granted, give them to me. I will make them more special than anything. Tell people who are white and Black they are automatically pretty. Be happy they're enough like you for you to finally understand something Black. Call me something other than Black. Teach me to be too be ashamed of my former names. Instead of negro, colored, African American tell me Nigga is just the same. Make me surly. Let's speed up what Darwin started. Take the best of us. Put us on a boat. Let the weak ones die. When the weak ones are dead, breed me with the largest and most agile buck. If you find me attractive, let's have babies, and hold our babies above all babies. Let me be light skinned and untarnished. Warn your children we are sons of Hamm. Cursed and cursing. Mutilate me, beat my back something awful and laugh at my calluses. Rape my woman in front of me, make laws that insure I can never call her my wife. Give the woman I am permitted to fuck in your absence children, treat them as livestock, treat them better than you treat her or me. Make a house Nigga out of your daughter. Willie Lynch me.

Beat me down and hang me off of trees. Confuse the hummingbird who does not know what to drink from. When I become aggressive, call me a thug. If I am complacent, tease me, call me sellout and remind me that I am not Black. Continue to always punish me, keep the written word a mystery and when I's don't speak good English too good, confront me. Tell me I am lazy, then have me walk 100 miles through the swamps of Mississippi in the dark alone. If I reject being lazy, have the dogs chase me. So I know what it feels like to be tired. When I'm tired, Rodney King me, play the tape and ask me not to be moved. If I am moved or become fearful of violence, watch me hurt myself and do nothing. Take my hurt, numb it with indifference. When I question my circumstance call it the race card, when you don't care what I am asking, ask for ID cards. Make me Black. Police flashlights in my face so often, I am only comfortable in the spotlight of a stage, arena, court, field or prison yard. Make me Black.

CLASSROOM GUIDE

Discuss the title, *Black Faggotry*. What does it reveal about the author and what does it ask of the reader? What does it means to be marginalized, biracial, Black, and finally, gay? How do these identities alter when they intersect? What cannot be changed or impacted through intersectionality? What never seems to change about the Black or the gay experience?

Identify which works are "spoken word" and which works are classified as "poetry." What is the difference between these two forms? Where has the author chosen either form, and why? Does the author allow himself to be more vulnerable for work that is designed for the page or the stage, and why might this be?

Use the following as prompts for free writes. Have the student write the prompt and continue writing until they have run out of things to say. Then have them write the prompt again. Repeat this action over and over for 5 minutes. It is important that the student does not stop writing during the 5 minutes. Prompts can include:

- Make Me Black/Make Me (fill in ethnicity)
- My Black Male Body/My (fill in gender identity, fill in ethnicity) Body

Using "The Atmosphere of a Dream," discuss what it means to be abstract. Define metaphor using common examples. Using metaphor in intentionally abstract ways, have the students describe in vivid detail what the atmosphere of a dream is.

Using "I Untitled," have your students complete the following sentences in the form of a template. Deviations should be encouraged. The template is a guide. This should result in a poem that is 24-or-more lines long.

I found, I found, I am finding
I sound, I sound, I am sounding
I see, I see, I am seeing
I feel, I feel, I am feeling
I taste, I taste, I am tasting
I smell, I smell, I am smelling
I hear, I hear, I am hearing
I am, I am, I be

ACKNOWLEDGEMENTS

I have been supported, inspired, held and pushed forward by such an amazing community of friends, family, peers and collaborators. So here goes...

First, I'd like to thank my mother Christine Lynn Carter for believing in me, especially when I didn't, and my father Lynn Edward Sykes for teaching me the power of words. Shout outs to my siblings, Danyale Smith, Alain Sykes, Damien Sykes, and David Gutteridge. To witness and be witnessed, you give my life and art value and meaning.

My chosen family: Elizabeth Jane Coleman for encouraging me to write and collect my first poems; Karen Difrummolo for making sure I would never be without the love of a mother; Colleen Hilker-Sykes for sticking with me during the difficult times; and Johnny Symons and William Rogers who have supported, challenged, and elevated me in every way possible.

The Miller-Handley Family, Aunt Lynn, Myshell, Mylisa, My Michael, My Isaac, and of course, My Derrick.

My queer family, ordered by appearance, not importance: Maya Cohen, Veleda Roehl, Ramona Webb, Rashad Pridgen, Nazelah Jamison, Ngaire Young, Kim Johnson, Valerie Trout, Audacious I Am, and Kierstin "My Maki" Gray.

Malia Byrne, Gabriel Christian, Jose Abod, Deirdre Visser, Shakiri, Zulfikar Ali Bhutto, Anne Bluethenthal, and the amazing Skywatchers Ensemble members.

Marvin K. White: You are the first person to have me read my poetry publicly. You taught me that Black Gay voices matter. I will always think of you in gratitude and celebrate the fact that after 20+ years, I still look up to you.

"Mama Calizo" Dwayne Patrick Calizo, Erika Chong Shuch, Zak Barnett. Anne Bluethenthal, Pam Peniston, Ellen Sebastien Chang, Mark Jackson, Carolyn Cooke, Cindy Shearer, and Brian Freeman—each of you nurtured and challenged me. I want to thank you for your many contributions during my artistic journey.

My mentees who have allowed me the privilege of giving back what has been given to me—Na Na Duffuor, Javier Stell-Fresquez, Ivy Monteiro, Gabriel Christian, and Chibueze Crouch.

Finally, I want to thank Nomadic Press and J. K. Fowler for providing me the opportunity to collect and express myself on the page. Poetry is the origin of all my creativity. The publication of *Black Faggotry* is an invitation for me to come home. So, I thank you.

DAZIÉ GREGO-SYKES is an Oakland, California, performance artist and poet. He is a graduate of The Experimental Performance Institute at New College of California. It was there he learned to transform spoken word into incendiary solo plays. Dazié also received his MFA in Interdisciplinary Arts and Writing from The California Institute of Integral Studies.

Dazié's first full-length solo performance *Am I A Man* is a multidisciplinary work that focuses on the ways in which gay men of color claim and hold their masculinity. *Am I A Man* has been a part of the National Queer Arts Festival and the Murmuration Festival at Z-Space in San Francisco and has been toured nationally in the United Solo Festival and Frigid Fringe Festival.

Dazié's most recent performance work titled *Nigga-Roo* was originally commissioned by the Queer Cultural Center and has been performed at The Marsh San Francisco, The Flight Deck in Oakland, and at The Exit Theater where he received the Best of Fringe Award in 2017.

www.ingramcontent.com/pod-product-compliance
Lightning Source LLC
Chambersburg PA
CBHW030001110526
44587CB00012BA/1210